sc√m

THE SCIENCE MUSEUM BOOK OF AMAZING FACTS

COMMUNICATIONS

Always fascinated by communications, Sarah Angliss decided to study sound and electronics when she left school. After working for a while as an engineer, Sarah joined the Science Museum where she had the opportunity to communicate her interests to others. Sarah now works at home, keeping in touch with museums and publishers by phone, fax, e-mail and the postbox around the corner. At the end of the working day, there's nothing she likes better than to communicate with her family and friends, face to face, over a nice cup of tea.

Many of the amazing facts in this book were inspired by exhibits in the SCIENCE MUSEUM in London. It is home to many of the greatest treasures in the history of science, invention and discovery, and there are also hands-on galleries where you can try things out for yourself. If you live in the North of England visit the Science Museum's outposts, the National Railway Museum in York and the National Museum of Photography, Film and Television in Bradford.

Published by Hodder Children's Books 1998
The right of Sarah Angliss to be identified as the Author and
the right of Christine Roche to be identified as the illustrator of the Work
has been asserted by them in accordance with the
Copyright, Designs and Patents Act 1988.

10 9 8 7 6 5 4 3 2

A Catalogue record for this book is available
from the British Library

ISBN 0 340 71475 1

Designed by Fiona Webb
Cover illustration by Ainslie MacLeod

Hodder Children's Books
A division of Hodder Headline
338 Euston Road
London NW1 3BH

Printed and bound in Great Britain by
The Guernsey Press Co. Ltd, Guernsey, Channel Islands

Sci √m

THE SCIENCE MUSEUM
BOOK OF AMAZING FACTS

COMMUNICATIONS

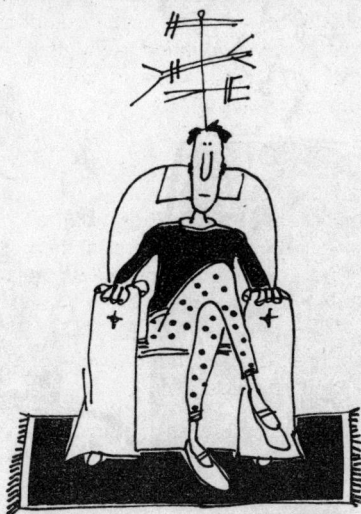

SARAH ANGLISS

ILLUSTRATED BY CHRISTINE ROCHE

𝒽

Hodder
Children's
Books

a division of Hodder Headline

Contents

WHEN WAS THE LAST TIME YOU SENT TWO MILLION WORDS OF TEXT PER SECOND?

CHAPTER 1

Person to person

It's never been easier to keep in touch. If you need to speak to someone over the other side of the world, all you have to do is pick up the telephone. If you're too shy to call, you can always post a letter, fax a document or send an e-mail.

Modern communications are easy to use — they're also incredibly swift. A telephone call can cross the Atlantic in a split second — in just over a second, it could reach the Moon. These facts are even more amazing when you remember the speed of messages a couple of centuries ago. Until the first telegraphs came along, messages could only travel as fast as they could be carried on horseback — or by ship. Distant battles could be won or lost weeks before people knew about them. Relatives who moved a few hundred kilometres away seemed as remote as those on another continent.

As modern communications let us keep in touch over any distance, people say we live in a 'global village'. However, very few of us get a chance to use the technology that lets us enjoy this new form of village life. There may be a billion telephones in the world — but they are only used by a third of the planet. Millions of people will never send a fax, write an e-mail or even make a telephone call in their lifetimes.

THE POSTAL SERVICE

FIRST POST

The oldest letter in Britain is an invitation to a birthday party. Sent by a Roman living there to his friend at Hadrian's Wall, the letter is about 1900 years old. The Roman postal service was so good, it could carry a letter from London to Cardiff in only three days. The Egyptians probably have the oldest postal service – it was started over 4000 years ago.

I'M INVITED TO A PARTY!

I'M INVITED TO A PARTY!

CASH ON DELIVERY

If you sent a letter in England before 1635, the King or Queen would have paid your postage. When charges were brought in, you had to pay for the letters you received, not for the ones you sent. As post was so expensive, people found all sorts of ways to avoid paying for it. For instance, they would check that a relative was alive and well by looking for their handwriting on an envelope. Once they had spotted it, they would refuse to actually pay for any of their letters.

HIGHWAY ROBBERY

It wasn't an easy life being a post boy – or post girl – 250 years ago. You had to deliver letters in all weathers, you were easy prey for highwaymen and you could be sentenced to hard labour if you were found carrying illegal mail. Riding on horseback, the post boys and girls were expected to travel over eight kilometres a day. In the winter, they packed their tin helmets and leather boots with straw to keep warm.

LETTER OF THE LAW

In the 1780s, death was the punishment for stealing letters. That didn't deter some highwaymen from ambushing mailcarts and post workers. That's why the Post Office published a leaflet in 1782 telling people to chop banknotes in half before they sent them in the post. If the two halves of a banknote were posted at different times, a highwayman wouldn't be able to use it.

THAT'S RICH

Only 150 years ago, it would have cost an entire week's wages to send a handful of letters just 100 kilometres. That's why only the rich could afford to use the post. As MPs (Members of

Parliament) were given free postage, some unscrupulous ones were made secretaries of different companies. The companies would have all their mail sent to and from their MP so they didn't have to pay a penny in postage.

LICKING THE PROBLEM

The first stamps were introduced along with the first cheap postage. In the early 1800s, more people moved to big cities or emigrated (went overseas) to distant countries. The British government realised they needed a cheap way to send letters so everyone could afford to keep in touch. In 1840, they brought in a service that let anyone send small letters for a penny. People were told to put a black sticker, which had a picture of the queen's head, on the front of their letters to prove they had already paid their postage. This sticker, called a Penny Black, is now a collectors' item.

FROM PILLAR TO POST

People were very wary about using post boxes when they first appeared in the 1850s. They found it hard to believe that it was safe to leave their letters all day long in a box that was out on the street. A famous novelist called Anthony

Trollope introduced the post box to Britain. When he wasn't writing books, Trollope worked as a surveyor for the Post Office. He was inspired to bring the post box to Britain after seeing it in use on the small island of Jersey.

SKY'S THE LIMIT

The first airmail service carried letters only twenty kilometres. Taking off on 9 September 1911, it flew post from one side of London to the other. The pilot, Gustav Hamel, ran the entire service using a tiny, one-seater Blériot aeroplane. By 1921, airmail was big business. Letters which normally took a month to reach Cairo from Baghdad could get there in only ten days by air. In the 1930s, special blue post boxes appeared that were specially for airmail. Although these used to be a regular sight on city streets, they have now all gone.

A WING AND A PRAYER

Plucky pigeons were a lifeline for the people of Paris in 1870. At that time, the city was under siege. People could only get messages out of the city by flying them out on the birds. Parisians photographed important messages,

then shrank the photographs to a fraction of their size using a brand-new process called 'microphotography'. They stuffed tiny microphotographs into a quill which they tied to a pigeon's tail feathers. Only one in twenty pigeons got out of Paris safely but each one carried no less than 3200 messages, packed on to sixteen microphotographs.

LITTLE THINGS MEAN A LOT

In World War II, cargo space was precious so troops' letters were sent home as microphotographs. This meant 1600 letters, which would normally make a bulky 20-kilogramme package, could be carried on one tiny reel of film. Once the film was flown home, it could be enlarged so loved ones could read their letters. After the war, Russia was desperately short of paper so schools were given microphotographs of text books. Teachers showed the books to the class by shining light through them, just like films. If you go to your local history library, you may find they store copies of old newspapers as microphotographs. This lets them pack the information from thousands of newspapers into a tiny space.

BLAST IT!

The first – and only – attempt to send ordinary letters by rocket went with a bang on 31 July 1934. Set up in Scotland by German rocket pioneer Gerhard Zucker, the *Western Isles Rocket Post* promised to deliver mail between the isles of Harris and Scarp in seconds. People who used the service were dismayed to find that the rocket blew up on takeoff.

EARLY TELEGRAPHS

HOT NEWS

In the 1580s, a chain of warning bonfires across Britain could send only two messages. One was 'Help! The Spanish invaders are coming!' and the other was 'Oh no! The Spanish invaders are here!'. Compare that to the clever system the Ancient Greeks put together over 2400 years ago. Using sets of five torches, it could send any letter of the Greek alphabet. The people who ran it burned different combinations of torches to send different letters. Although it must have been quite slow, the Ancient Greeks were able to use this system on every hilltop to send detailed messages from town to town.

SCHOOLBOY NOTES

A French schoolboy, Claude Chappe, went to great lengths to send messages to his brother. Using two wooden arms mounted on a long, high pole, he put together a system that could send thousands of different words. Chappe could tilt the two arms at different angles just by turning some handles. Different arm positions stood for different words. As the arms were high up in the air, his brother could see them even if he was a few hundred metres away. Claude's brother knew the code that was used to send different words. He could look at the positions of the arms to work out the message that Claude had sent. In the 1770s, Chappe gave his invention to the French revolutionaries. This system, called semaphore, was also adopted by the British who used it to keep in touch about the Battle of Waterloo.

THE ELECTRIC TELEGRAPH

GASSING AWAY

German inventor Samuel Soemmering wanted people to read messages in bubbles. He first floated his idea, the bubble telegraph, in 1810.

A telegraph is a system that can send messages over long distances. Most telegraphs send messages from one place to another through wires. People started to look for ways to make a telegraph system soon after the earliest experiments with electricity took place in the mid eighteenth century. Samel Soemmering's invention used electricity to make pockets of gas bubble up in a tank of acid. Soemmering had 26 different wires sitting in the acid, one for each letter of the alphabet. If he sent a small current of electricity down any of the wires, a stream of bubbles would appear from it. This is how he was able to send messages, one letter at a time.

OLD NEWS

Before telegraph systems came along, distant battles could be won or lost weeks before anyone found out about them. The only messaging systems around, like semaphore and bonfires (*see* **Hot news** *page 14 and* **Schoolboy notes** *page 15)*, took a long time to relay just a few words. They sent these messages no more than a few hundred metres at a time – to the next hill for example. Over much longer distances, messages could only travel as fast as they could be carried on horseback – or by ship. One of the most successful early telegraphs was invented by William Cooke and Charles Wheatstone around 1837. Cooke and Wheatstone's telegraph used changes in the electricity across a wire to move a needle around a dial. Their 'needle telegraph' used five or six different needles. Two needles moved at a time, pointing to a letter on a grid behind them. Early telegraphs like this were often used to send messages between railway stations. This helped railway companies to write more accurate timetables and to make train journeys safer.

A FINE DASH

It was a painter, not an engineer, who brought us a simple code that could be used to send telegraph messages really swiftly. The painter in question, a young man called Samuel Morse, borrowed his idea from the American engineer Alfred Vail. Morse's telegraph could send any letter of the alphabet using a series of long and short pulses of electricity – dots and dashes. By 1866, a telegraph line stretched across the Atlantic, allowing people in Britain and America to keep in regular touch by telegraph. Using a

code based on Morse's dots and dashes, people could send detailed messages across the ocean in minutes.

WALK THE LINE

Mending telegraph lines was so dangerous, people who did this could hardly ever get life insurance. Every large telegraph company employed 'linesmen' – people who were paid to walk the route of the telegraph lines, checking and fixing any faults. Linesmen, who had to work in all weathers, were often seen 'walking the line' in open fields and prairies. If they weren't electrocuted by telegraph cables, they were often struck by lightning. Covered in the tar they used to stop the lines from rusting, the unfortunate linesmen were often banned from inns along the line.

GOING UNDERGROUND

The telegraph caused chaos in cities in the 1880s. As doctors, surveyors and merchants all had their own systems, the skyline was one great rats' nest of wires. A typical city street would be cluttered with telegraph poles. Every pole would have 25 arms and every arm would carry up to 250 wires. Over the next forty years, things gradually improved. People put some telegraph cables underground and began to send some Morse code messages by radio instead (see **That sinking feeling** *below and* **Recipe for success** *page 34*)

THAT SINKING FEELING

'SOS from MGJ – We have struck an iceberg sinking fast come to our assistance.' One of the most famous Morse code messages of all time, this desperate plea for help was sent by radio on 14 April 1912 by the radio operator of the great ship *Titanic*.

As the *Titanic* sank into the icy waters of the Arctic Ocean, the radio operator kept at his station, sending the SOS signal to attract other ships. Although 1513 men, women and children drowned, his message helped to save many other lives.

The first-ever message to use the SOS signal, it fired the world's imagination about the new invention called 'wireless telegraph' – Morse code sent by radio.

BIGGEST MACHINE IN THE WORLD

THINK BIG

What's the biggest machine on Earth? If you think it's something like a supertanker or nuclear power plant, you may be surprised to hear it's the telephone system. A vast network of cables and satellites link together a billion different telephones, fax machines and modems that let a third of the world keep in touch.

LONG DISTANCE

WATCH YOUR LANGUAGE NEIL — IT'S THE PRESIDENT ON THE 'PHONE —

The furthest long-distance phone call ever was between two people over a third of a million kilometres apart. The historic chat, on 24 July 1969, took place between US President Richard Nixon and American astronauts Neil Armstrong and Buzz Aldrin. Nixon, who was phoning from the White House, spoke to Armstrong and Aldrin while they were on the Moon. As they spoke of their wish for world peace, 600 million people listened in on TVs and radios around the world. Many thought the astronauts were speaking slowly because they were overcome with emotion. In fact, they were simply making sure they didn't say anything stupid on the most expensive and public phone call ever.

FAST TALKING

Messages travel through a telephone system amazingly fast. It takes only a fraction of a second for a telephone signal to travel from London to New York. When you use a telephone, a microphone inside it picks up the sound of your voice and turns it into an electrical signal. This signal travels along telephone lines at an incredible 20,000 kilometres per second – that's two-thirds the speed of light. The biggest hold-ups on a telephone system are inside the computers that boost telephone signals, turn them into digital signals (see **Done with numbers** *below*) or chop them up so it can share a line (see **Private conversation** *page 39*). Even these tasks only delay the signal by a few millionths of a second. Sound travels through air about 600,000 times slower than a telephone signal travels along a cable. So, in the time it takes your voice to travel a few centimetres to the handset of a telephone, a telephone signal can travel about 60 kilometres.

THE DIGITAL ADVANTAGE

DONE WITH NUMBERS

If you could plug a telephone in half way along the most modern kind of telephone cable, all you'd hear would be a strange hiss. That's because the line doesn't carry an ordinary telephone signal. Instead, it carries lots of amazingly short pulses of electricity – or, in the case of optical fibres, light (see **Light fantastic** *page 24*). These pulses would make a hiss if they were turned back into sound by a telephone. They are made in an instant by computers in telephone exchanges – places that sort out all the telephone calls that are being made and send them along the right lines.

The pulses from a telephone exchange send numbers from one end of the cable to the other, just like the dots and dashes that make up Morse code send letters. The signal that is made up of pulses is called a 'digital signal'. The numbers sent by the pulses show the size of the telephone signal every instant – thousands of pulses are sent for one phone call in a single second. Once the pulses reach the other end of the wire, another computer turns them back into an ordinary signal that we can hear as proper speech on a telephone.

CRACKING THE CRACKLES

A digital signal is a crackle-free signal. That's why telephone companies go to all the bother of making ordinary electrical signals digital (*see* **Done with numbers** *page 22*). When an ordinary telephone message goes along a copper wire, any stray signals on the wire mix with the telephone signal, making it hiss and crackle. These stray signals come from nearby machines, other cables or from local thunderstorms. If a signal is digital, it is sent as a series of pulses. Only a really big stray signal will make it impossible to tell when a pulse is being sent. So a digital signal is hardly affected by stray signals at all. Telephone systems aren't the only things that make the most of digital technology. CD players (see **Making tracks** *page 53*, **In a spin** *page 53, and* **Sounds perfect** *page 54*) also store sound digitally. They store the pulses that make up a digital signal as a series of tiny pits. That's why they sound crystal clear.

LIGHT FANTASTIC

These days, when you talk on the telephone, your call is probably carried along cables made of glass. Telephone calls are sent along glass fibres as pulses of light. In other words, they are sent 'digitally' (see **Done with numbers** *page 22*). Amazingly, the light stays in the glass, even when the cable goes around corners.
A glass fibre can carry many more messages than an ordinary copper wire. Because it carries light, not electricity, its signal is not affected in any way by stray electrical signals from nearby machines, cables or lightning storms (see **Cracking crackles** *page 23*). So a telephone signal sent along a glass fibre is the most hiss- and crackle-free of all.

TELEPHONE INVENTIONS AND INVENTORS

A CLOSE CALL

THE TELEPHONE WAS A NICE IDEA, MR GRAY, BUT YOU'RE 7 HOURS TOO LATE, I'M AFRAID.

PATENT OFFICER

Imagine how mad you would be if you'd missed being the inventor of something by just a few hours. Well, that's what happened to Elisha Gray, an unfortunate inventor of the telephone. On 7 March 1876, Gray wrote an official note explaining how to make a telephone. This note was filed at a 'patent office', a place where people officially register, claim and date their inventions. Some time later, he found that another inventor, Alexander Graham Bell, had patented roughly the same idea only seven hours before him. Gray took this stroke of bad luck amazingly well – probably because he thought there was more money to be made in the telegraph than the telephone.

STORM IN A TEACUP?

HELLO...

Country blacksmith Daniel Drawbaugh claimed he used a teacup to make a telephone in 1867 – nine years before Bell. Although he won public sympathy, he was unable to prove his story in court. A German school teacher, Philip Reis, had a similar problem. Claims that he built the first telephone from a violin case, a stretched sausage skin and a hollowed-out beer-barrel bung were rejected because he couldn't make his device work in the witness box. In a desperate bid to get the court to believe him, one of Reis' lawyers explained 'it can speak, but it won't'. Dismissing his efforts, a judge said 'a century of Reis would never produce a working telephone'. Sadly, it was almost certainly true that Reis *did* get his telephone to work after a fashion around 1861. There are records of him using his telephone at his school as early as 1862 – fourteen years before Bell.

FIRST WORDS

'Mr Watson, come here, I want you!'
These unremarkable words were the first ever heard on Bell's telephone. Bell's early telephone was so basic, one part had to work as both the bit you speak into and the bit you listen to. As

Bell's advertisements explained, 'much trouble is caused by both parties speaking at the same time. When you are not speaking, you should be listening.' Although these were the first words spoken on Bell's system, they may not be the first words ever spoken on the telephone (see **Storm in a teacup** page 26).

NUMBER PLEASE!

An undertaker's concern about losing business to a rival led to the invention of the automatic telephone exchange. Until Almon Brown Strowger had invented the automatic exchange, people couldn't dial numbers directly. They had to ask operators to put them through. Strowger was fed up with the rudeness of these operators and with all the time he had to wait while they put him through to customers. Worse still, he knew his business was suffering because his rival's girlfriend worked as an operator. When people rang up with new business for Strowger, she put them through to his rival's firm. Keen to save his business, Strowger developed a system that would put callers through to other numbers automatically. Strowger's system replaced human operators with an automatic machine that was controlled and powered by electricity.

It worked so well, it was soon adopted throughout the world, putting thousands of telephone operators out of a job. Strowger called it 'the girl-less, cuss-less phone' ('cussing' means swearing). Today, most of Strowger's exchanges have been replaced by computerised ones.

SHOP AROUND THE CLOCK

'On-line shopping' may sound like a new idea – but it's almost as old as the telephone itself. As early as 1902, the science fiction writer H.G. Wells suggested housewives could order goods over the phone. By 1906, thousands of stores had telephone ordering services – some working around the clock.

These days, on-line shopping lets you do more than simply order goods. Anyone who's lucky enough to own a computer, modem and credit card can also look at goods and pay for them – all from the comfort of their own home.

Supermarkets can even work out which groceries on-line customers like to buy, then do their weekly shopping for them.

A MATTER OF TASTE

In 1910, a magazine suggested it may one day be possible to see, feel and even taste over the telephone. Although people tried to make video phones as early as 1902, live pictures weren't sent over phone lines until 1927. These days, for the cost of the average television, you can buy a video phone that plugs into an ordinary phone socket. If a top-notch doctor is very busy, he or she may see you over a video phone – rather than in person.

IT'S MY FOOT, DOC....

VIRTUALLY CORRECT

AND I'M WARNING YOU—
I'M WEARING MY
DATAGLOVE!

When people predicted we could touch over the telephone, they weren't too wide of the mark. Over the last ten years, two things have been developed that allow us to feel by phone. One is the 'dataglove', a mitten that's covered with fine air pockets. When you wear a dataglove, you feel as though you are touching something

when air is blown into its air pockets. The other development is the Internet, the network that lets people send messages by computer (*see* **Web of war** *page 34 and* **Home work** *page 77*). Two people wearing datagloves can literally keep in touch over the Internet. If someone wants to hold their friend's hand for example, they have to curl up their own hand, as if their friend's hand was really there. Their dataglove will send messages to their friend's dataglove over the Internet, telling it they have done this. When this happens, the friend's data-glove will fill up with air, squeezing their hand.

OTHER WAYS TO USE THE TELEPHONE

GET THE FAX

A fax machine uses up to six million dots to copy something on a page. When you put a printed page in a fax machine, it looks at the page in minute detail and works out which parts of the page are covered in ink. It works down the page, looking at one thin line of the page at a time. It makes a series of pulses that can travel over a telephone line, telling another fax machine how each tiny part of the line is

different from the one above it. This is a type of 'digital signal' (see **Done with numbers** *page 22*). A fax machine at the other end of a telephone line can pick up these pulses and use them to make a copy of the page.

GLOBAL VILLAGE

These days, you can send a written message anywhere in the world for the cost of a local phone call. To do this, you need 'e-mail' – a system that lets computers send messages to each other over the phone. When you e-mail someone thousands of kilometres away, you only have to telephone a special computer down the road. That computer sends your message long-distance on your behalf. It's not only written words that you can send by e-mail. You can also send pictures, videos, sound and anything else that can be stored on a computer. Computers phone each other up using 'modems' – devices that convert their messages into pulses that can travel along phone lines. The signals from a modem are digital signals (see **Done with numbers** *page 22*). If you could plug your telephone into the phone line between the modems, all you would hear is a long hiss.

WEB OF WAR

When you consider how easily we can use e-mail these days, it's odd to think about its secretive origins. E-mail travels on a giant world-wide network of computers called the Internet. This is the descendent of another network called Arpanet. The Pentagon, America's military headquarters, set up Arpanet in 1969. They wanted it to be a war-proof messaging system.

Secret messages could be chopped into different pieces then sent along separate parts of Arpanet, making them harder to spy on. If any part of Arpanet was wiped out by a nuclear bomb, surviving parts of the network would still offer plenty of different routes for sending vital information.

ON THE MOVE

RECIPE FOR SUCCESS

Microwaves aren't only good for cooking food – they're also good for sending messages. In fact, microwave ovens have only been around for about 30 years but microwaves have been used to send messages for over a century.

WHEN WAS THE LAST TIME YOU SENT TWO MILLION WORDS OF TEXT PER SECOND?

Microwaves are very like radio waves but are much easier to focus on to a narrow target like a small aerial on a ship. Heinrich Hertz, the first person to send waves like these through the air, used microwaves in his early experiments. Guglielmo Marconi, the first person to send Morse code by radio, also experimented with microwaves (see **A fine dash** *page 17* and **That sinking feeling** *page 19*). In 1924, a friend of Marconi, C.S. Franklin, used microwaves to send a telephone message from England to Australia. By the 1930s, people used microwaves regularly to carry telephone calls from mainland Britain to nearby islands like Stornaway, Castlebay and Guernsey. Mobile phones today still use low-powered microwaves – so do some portable computers. Microwaves can be used to send up to two million words of text a second. Compare that to a semaphore system – it could only send a dozen words in that time.

ALWAYS GOOD TO KEEP IN TOUCH?

HAND DELIVERED

In the 1870s, many rich people in Britain thought the phone would never catch on as they already had servants to deliver their messages. Around that time, city streets would be crammed with messenger boys – young men who would run between offices and houses, delivering letters and telegrams by hand (telegrams are urgent letters sent by the telegraph). Many boys left school early to make a living as a messenger. When asked why the telephone had caught on in America, a leading engineer, Sir William Preece explained 'the absence of servants has compelled Americans to adopt communications systems'.

DIAL 'M' FOR MADNESS

As a dire warning to would-be phone users, a German psychiatrist reported that at least one patient had been driven mad by using the phone. In 1912, he cautioned 'excitable persons ... should never use the telephone'. Some religious people had even sterner words about the phone. They ordered their followers not to use the new 'device of Satan' as it would make them lazy.

HOW DEPRESSING!

The phone hasn't always made life richer – in fact, it was partly responsible for the biggest economic depression of the century. In 1929, traders in Wall Street, New York, had a day of panic selling when share prices started to plummet.

Shares tell you how much companies or their goods are worth – the lower the price of shares, the worse off a company is. As share prices fell, traders jumped on to the new telephone system to sell them faster than ever before. This rapidly brought the value of goods to an all-time low, triggering the Depression of the 1930s.

BLACK MONDAY

A new way to keep in touch caused another economic depression in the 1980s. On a day now known as Black Monday, share prices started falling on London's Stock Exchange so some new computer equipment kicked into action. Different computers started phoning each other up, trading shares automatically. Traders had to watch helplessly as the computer trading wiped billions of pounds off the value of shares in just a few hours.

GUIDE TO SNOOPING

SURPRISE PARTY

Until the 1970s, many callers had to be wary about discussing private matters on the phone. That's because they had 'party lines' – cheap telephone lines that they shared with other people in the street. Nosy neighbours could simply pick up their phone to eavesdrop on their calls. In 1912, a woman living in the US countryside told a newspaper how her party line kept her cheery. When she felt lonely, she would pick up the phone, catch scraps of other's conversations, and offer other callers advice!

PRIVATE CONVERSATION?

Although we don't have to suffer party lines any more, we do still share telephone lines with over 50,000 other callers. When you make a phone call, the signal from your telephone call goes to a telephone exchange (see **Done with numbers** page 22). To cram your phone call and lots of others on to just one line, the telephone exchange chops every call up into a stream of tiny pieces – each just a fraction of a second long. They can then send each piece, along with snatches of thousands of other calls, along a single cable. When signals reach their destination, exchanges put the pieces back together to make thousands of separate, complete calls. These are sent along separate wires to the phones receiving the calls. This technique, called 'multiplexing', works so well, callers are completely unaware of the fact that it's happening.

ANYTHING BUGGING YOU?

A bug the size of a cocktail olive can let you snoop on an entire room. A 'bug' is the nickname for a device that let's you secretly snoop on people's conversations. The art of making and using bugs is called 'surveillance'.

A few years ago, Hal Lipset, a surveillance expert from San Francisco, USA, slipped a tiny microphone into a thin copper tube about one centimetre long. He poured plastic around the tube then painted it green so it looked like an olive. After disguising the bug's aerial as a cocktail stick, he slipped the whole thing into someone's drink.

CRAWLING WITH BUGS

The American embassy in Moscow used to be one huge bug. When the embassy was built, the Soviet government asked builders to pour thousands of electronic devices – called 'diodes' – into the concrete. These would confuse any bug detector, making it impossible to track down any of the hundreds of real bugs in the building. Even the embassy's typewriters were bugged – they constantly monitored which keys were being pressed.

SPY GLASS

You don't need a bug within a room to snoop on the people inside it – a window pane will do. Simply shine a laser beam at the window so it's reflected by the window pane. Then wait for people in the room to speak. The sounds of their voices will make the window pane vibrate, so your reflected beam will bounce to and fro. With the right equipment, you can monitor your bouncing beam and use its movement to recreate the sound in the room. Next time you feel like someone's bugging you – you could be right.

Quiz

1 The oldest letter in Britain is
   a) a birthday invitation
   b) a water bill
   c) a love letter

2 Post boys and girls were sentenced to hard labour if they were
   caught
   a) smoking a cigarette
   b) carrying illegal post
   c) not wearing the uniform

3 In 1810, Samuel Soemmering found a way to send messages
   a) by making bubbles
   b) by flying a trained parrot
   c) by shouting underwater

4 The biggest machine on Earth is
   a) the railway network
   b) the Panama canal
   c) the telephone network

5 The furthest long-distance telephone call ever took place between
   a) The North and South Poles
   b) Earth and the Moon
   c) Mars and Jupiter

6   Fed up with losing business to a rival, an undertaker invented
    a) a telephone answering machine
    b) an automatic telephone exchange
    c) a conveyor belt

7   In the 1870s, people thought the telephone wouldn't catch on because
    a) servants could deliver notes
    b) people were worried about being bugged
    c) it was too difficult to use

8   A dataglove lets you
    a) privately check up on useful facts
    b) 'touch' people over long distances
    c) keep germs at bay when using public telephones

9   Share prices in Britain plummeted on a day called
    a) Ash Wednesday
    b) First Tuesday
    c) Black Monday

10 Surveillance expert Hal Lipset is famous for hiding a bug in
    a) a Yorkshire terrier
    b) a desk lamp
    c) a cocktail olive

CHAPTER 2
Sounds great

These days, almost all the music we hear is on CDs, records, tapes and the radio. Recorded music is the norm — we only hear music 'live' on special occasions or when we pay to go to a gig or concert.

Sound recording has enabled us to have music on tap. We can take it anywhere, play it at any volume and even listen to it in the background. Since sound recording was invented, the quality of recordings has improved beyond belief. A century ago, recordings were so poor, people listening to them could scarcely make out which instruments were playing. These days, the best recordings are crystal clear. They let us hear every detail of a performance — even the breathing of a musician or the turning of a page. It's 'live' music today, with the occasional fluff on stage and noise from the audience, that has to struggle to keep up with many people's experience of recorded sound.

Sound technology has enabled more of us than ever to enjoy listening to the music we love. Sadly though, CDs, tapes and old-style vinyl records are all slowly decaying. The music on them is gradually fading away. Unless someone keeps recopying music on to new, perfect CDs or tapes, there's no hope that it will last forever.

OUR SOUND SYSTEM

ALL EARS

Our ears can hear a pin drop, even though its sound is a billion times less powerful than the sound of a car horn. We hear sounds when something makes the air around us vibrate. The faster the air vibrates, the higher the sound it makes. Our ears can only hear vibrations that wobble to and fro faster than twenty times but slower than twenty thousand times a second. Dogs can hear vibrations that happen up to thirty thousand times a second. That's why you can call a dog with a whistle that's far too high for a human to hear.

GOOD VIBRATIONS

Whales don't need telephones – they keep in touch over thousands of kilometres just by vibrating the seawater. The patterns of the vibrations are really complex – as though they form some kind of language. Whales wobble the water to and fro no faster than twenty times a second. Although we can't hear vibrations as slow as this, we can feel them. Some people buy giant speakers, called 'subwoofers' that can make sounds like this. These let them enjoy the feel of very low sounds that vibrate the whole room – and shake their bodies.

SOUND IDEAS

MUSIC TO THEIR EARS?

When a reporter heard a violin and piano playing on one of the first record players, he could tell when the violin stopped and started – but he couldn't tell much else. He found it hard to believe another engineer who said he'd been moved to tears by the beautiful sounds the machine made. Built in 1877, the first music machine, a 'phonograph', was designed by

Thomas Edison. It recorded sound on a sheet of tin foil that was stuck to the outside of a brass cylinder. Although Edison was the first person to get a music machine to work, it was a French inventor, Charles Cros, who had first worked out how to record sound.

EARLY RECORDINGS

Very special talents were needed to make some of the earliest music recordings. Singers had to roll their 'rs' and pronounce every 's' as a 'sh' to get words across. That's because, until the late 1920s, recordings were made without microphones. A band could only record a song by playing into a giant horn that funnelled sound on to a tiny sheet of metal. As the band played, the sheet vibrated and moved a needle that cut a wax disk. The disk could then be copied to make records. Instruments like drums and double basses didn't record at all well on this system. They were replaced by banjos and brass instruments which recorded much better.

WITH STRINGS ATTACHED

One of the silliest early record players had built-in strings so listeners could join in with their favourite tunes. Built in 1908, the Klingsor had strings stretched across the front of its horn like a harp. Designed to 'disseminate (spread) the sound in every direction of the room', all the strings really did was attract dust. Owners were advised they could add a piano keyboard to the Klingsor so they could play along as they listened to it. In this respect it wasn't that different from the Karaoke machines that are used for sing-alongs today. Amazingly, the Klingsor sold well for about ten years.

SOUND OF SILENCE

'The talkies' (films with sound) didn't appear until 1927 – but films before then were far from silent. When you went to see an early film, a presenter called the 'master of ceremonies' would read out any words and fill in details of the plot. Specially-employed drama companies, with names like Actologue and Dramatone, would hide behind the screen and speak the actors' lines. Fancy machines, like the Noiseograph and Dramagraph, would add sound effects to the action.

SOUND THINKING?

In the 1920s, many musicians thought people would reject 'talking pictures'. In July 1929, one musician wrote 'it remains to be seen whether, when the novelty wears off, the patrons of theatres will be satisfied with this de-humanised form of entertainment'. It's not surprising that musicians didn't approve of 'the talkies' – they were putting lots of them out of a job. The first film sound was really bad because it was supplied on a record. The record never played in perfect time with the film so the overall effect was really awful. Eventually, film studios started putting sound tracks directly on to the film itself. This huge improvement, which stopped the film and the sound from getting out of step, made sure talking pictures were here to stay.

HIDDEN DEPTHS

Lots of male singers owe their career to a problem caused by a certain piece of equipment: the ribbon microphone. The main part of a ribbon is made of two thin, lightweight metal strips. If you sing into the microphone, these strips move nearer and further from a magnet, making an electric current. This current can be used to record the sound on record, CD or tape. When a singer gets very close to a ribbon microphone, something goes wrong. It makes the bass sounds (deep ones) in their voices much louder than the treble sounds (squeaky ones). Because of this, the ribbon microphone seems to flatter men's voices – it can bring out hidden depths in even the weediest singer. 'Crooners' like Bing Crosby and Nat King Cole both used ribbon microphones to help them sound mellow – the deep-voiced soul singer Barry White sometimes uses one today.

CYCLE SELLERS' SIDELINE

As early record players were made of lots of moving parts, many were sold in bicycle shops. In Britain, some would-be purchasers were put off by this – they thought bicycle sellers weren't artistic enough to sell such a product. Machines that could play cylindrical phonographs and flat gramophone records were both available in the early 1900s. However, they were all so expensive, shops had a hard time selling them. Some companies tried to attract more business by selling cheap, imported players that were dressed up with grand-sounding names like Monarch, Baron and Marquis.

HEARING DOUBLE

LATERAL THINKING

People were thinking about stereo sound only four years after Edison made the first sound recording (*see* **Music to their ears?** *page 46*).

In 1881, an inventor called Clement Ader suggested that people could listen to opera over the telephone. For best effect, he recommended listening through two telephones – one relaying sounds from the left-hand side of the stage and one relaying sounds from the right. This suggestion, which would have produced stereo sound, wasn't tried for another 40 years.

IN EARSHOT

The first stereo sound system was used for the grim task of tracking enemy aircraft. In World War I, two giant listening trumpets were connected by tubes to a soldier's ears. As a plane moved overhead, the soldier would be able to hear the sound of its engine move from one ear to the other.

TAPES AND CDs

HIGHLY STRUNG

Listening to the first 'tape' recorder was a dangerous operation. Rather than tape, the 'telegraphon' stored sound on a taut, steel piano wire. The wire, which whizzed around at a hair-raising two metres per second, often snapped, causing untold damage to any objects – or people – nearby. Invented by Valdemar Poulsen in 1893, the telegraphon used magnetism to store sound. As someone spoke into its microphone, it magnetised different parts of the steel wire, storing sound. Modern cassette tapes, which appeared in 1962, store sound in roughly the same way. They are covered in magnetised granules of rust.

MAKING TRACKS

Sound on a CD is stored on a spiral track that's over six kilometres long. A CD stores sounds digitally (see **Done with numbers** *page 22*). The track of a CD is made of millions of tiny pits, each just a millionth of a metre wide. That's a hundredth of the width of a human hair – and a hundredth of the width of the groove of an ordinary vinyl record. The pits on a CD are so tiny, they can only be read by a fine beam of laser light. The laser reflects differently from pitted and flat areas of the disk. The CD player, which notices when the laser reaches a pit, turns the information stored on the disk into sound.

IN A SPIN

The spiral groove of a record is played from its edge to its middle – but the pits on a CD are played the other way round. A record player spins LPs (records that last about half an hour on each side) a steady 33⅓ times a minute. A CD player spins CDs at a varying rate. When a laser is reading the centre of a CD, a CD spins 500 times a minute. When its reads the edge, the CD spins only 200 times a minute.

SOUNDS PERFECT

It's possible – in theory at least – to play a CD after you've drilled a two-millimetre hole right through it. That's because every CD contains extra pits that help it play properly. A CD player uses the information stored in these extra pits to check it hasn't misread any other parts of the CD. If the CD player spots an error, it smooths it over so we hardly notice it. About a third of the space on every CD is taken up with these error-checking pits. Because of them, you rarely hear noises created by small scratches or lumps of dirt on a CD.

NOT A SCRATCH

In October 1982, American songwriter Billy Joel made history. His album, *52nd Street*, became the first-ever music you could buy on CD. Lots of music lovers were keen to find out more about CDs – after all, in the early 1980s, people thought CDs were indestructible. News reports showed CDs working even after they'd been smeared with jam! Fifteen years on, we know that CDs don't stand up well to such rough treatment. Although they do pick up less scratches than vinyl records, even CDs last longer if they're treated with tender loving care.

SPOILING THE FUN

Although they don't make any noise, there may be pits added to your favourite CD that stop you from copying it. Manufacturers have starting putting in pits like these, called 'spoilers', because they're worried that it's getting too easy to pirate music (illegally copy it on the cheap). Already, for a few hundred pounds, anyone can buy a machine that can record CDs from scratch. It uses a laser to burn pits into cheap, blank CDs, known as WORMs (WORM stands for Write Once Read Many times). To make matters worse for the manufacturers, it's now also possible to buy DAT tapes – digital cassette tapes that sound as good as CDs but can be recorded over many times (you can find out what 'digital' means in **Done with numbers** *page 22*). When you try to copy a CD with a spoiler, you'll get an earful of nasty noises that will ruin your recording.

NOTHING LASTS FOREVER

CREEPY!

If you went back to your treasured vinyl records after shelving them for a few centuries, you'd be in for a nasty shock. Where your row of lovely vinyl disks used to be, you'd probably be faced with a thick, black sludge. That's because the vinyl would slowly 'creep'. Just like a very gooey liquid, vinyl is continually running downhill to form puddles. This usually happens far too slowly for us to notice – but in hot weather it can happen alarmingly fast. Whatever the weather, vinyl records that are stored vertically will always end up slightly thicker at the bottom than at the top. That means over time their sound quality will slowly decay.

NOT FADE AWAY

Never bring a magnet near an audio tape. If you do, you'll wipe any sound that's stored on it. That's because the surface of an audio tape is covered in fine granules of rust. The granules act like tiny magnets. At each point of the tape, these tiny magnets record the strength of a tiny snatch of the sound. The louder the sound, the more the magnetism of the granules. If you bring a magnet too close to a tape, it will replace the granules' magnetic pattern with its own, wiping the tape. Sadly, lots of memorable tape recordings from the 1960s are already starting to fade. Magnets in nearby machines – and even the Earth's own magnetism – are slowly wiping their sound away.

ON AIR

HEARING VOICES

In 1906, people working on a ship were astounded to hear strange voices coming from nowhere. In their headphones, they had picked up the first-ever radio broadcasts of the human voice. As they'd never heard a radio programme before – it's no wonder they were puzzled by what they could hear. The broadcast had been made by a Canadian engineer, R.A. Fessenden. He'd put it together on equipment that was so basic, he burnt his lips if he got too close to his microphone.

LET'S BE SERIOUS

In Britain before the 1920s, radio entertainment was strictly out of the question. Thanks to the pioneering work of Guglielmo Marconi (see **Recipe for success** page 34) people had known how to broadcast radio waves since 1896. However, they were only allowed to use the radio for 'scientific research ... or general public utility' – mainly sending Morse code messages. By the 1920s, many people were ignoring this and using the radio to make their own news reports, plays, music and comedy shows. Eventually, the British government had to give in to public pressure and allow people to broadcast these sorts of things officially. For the first time ever, radio was allowed to become serious fun.

THE CAT'S WHISKERS

When the first radio shows went on air in Leeds, people were buying radio sets as fast as companies could make them. The first home radios were fairly primitive – no radio set was complete without its 'cat's whisker', a thin metal wire that touched a piece of crystal. The wire and crystal were connected to a giant aerial that had to be strung around the garden like an unruly washing line. The aerial picked up radio signals and turned them into tiny electric currents that vibrated to and fro. The cat's whisker managed to get rid of every part of this signal except the bit that could be used to make a sound. This sound was so tiny, it could only be heard through headphones. Things improved in the late 1920s when people could buy valves – electronic devices in glass bulbs that amplified the signals the radios made (in other words, made them louder).

RADIO COSY

If you had over £2000 to spare in 1959, you could buy a radio that had its own mink coat. Radio technology hadn't really improved over the last twenty years, so manufacturers came up with all sorts of gimmicks to sell more sets. Some, like Ecko, came up with affordable radios in sleek, ultramodern designs. Others, like Roberts, who brought the world the mink-coated radio, made expensive sets with high glamour. It wasn't until the late 1950s, when the transistor was mass produced, that radios started to change. The transistor, a tiny replacement for bulky valves (see **The cat's whiskers** page 58), meant radios could be made smaller than ever before.

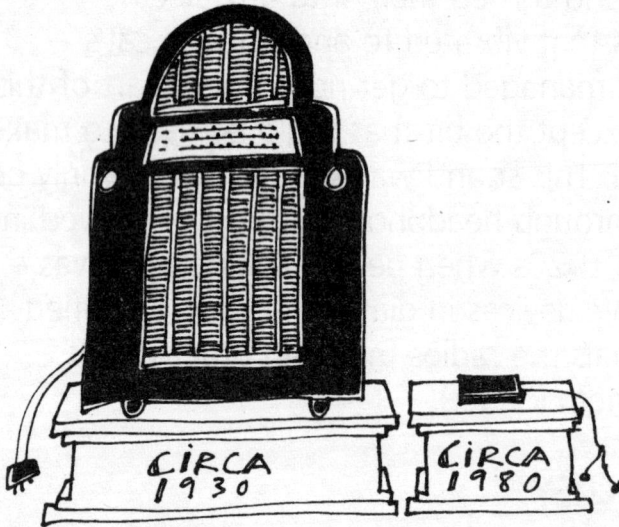

CIRCA 1930

CIRCA 1980

TINY TRANNIES

These days, we can squeeze about a million transistors into the space that only one took up in 1960. That's because we can etch millions of microscopic transistors on to a wafer of silicon

to make a microchip. Now, the buttons, batteries and loudspeaker are the largest parts of any radio. A brand new type of radio that uses microchip technology is coming along very soon. This radio will pick up digital broadcasts – ones that send information in a similar way to a CD. Digital broadcasts will be far clearer than anything we have heard so far. They may also be able to send pictures and text. We'll be able to see these on a mini-screen that's part of our digital radio – that's if we can afford one.

Quiz

1 Whales keep in touch
   a) by blinking their eyes
   b) by vibrating sea water
   c) by leaving scents

2 Many people bought the Klingsor record player because they liked its special
   a) strings
   b) headphones
   c) resonant legs

3 Lots of male singers owe their careers to
   a) a faulty microphone
   b) false teeth that whistle
   c) the slimming effect of television

4 In 1881, Clement Ader suggested people use pairs of telephones to listen
   a) to their heartbeat
   b) to the opera
   c) to football matches

5 Signals on CDs that stop you recording them are called
   a) spoilers
   b) howlers
   c) woofers

5 If you left a vinyl record on a shelf for hundreds of years, it would
   a) explode
   b) form a sludge
   c) turn see-through

7 Until the 1920s, it was illegal in Britain to use radio waves
   a) for entertainment
   b) for cooking
   c) for hypnosis

8 No early radio was complete without
   a) a cat's whisker
   b) a bee's knee
   c) a pig's ear

9 In 1959, you could buy a radio that had its own
   a) fan club
   b) mink coat
   c) radio station

10 Radios shrank in size when people started building them with
   a) plastic
   b) robots
   c) transistors

CHAPTER 3
In black and white

Few people would have been able to afford this book if it had been written by hand. Amazingly though, until an invention called 'moveable type' came along 500 years ago, this was the easiest way that people could put books together. Moveable type lets people print lots of copies of a book very quickly and easily — you can find out exactly what it is on page 72. Moveable type may have made books cheaper but books remained too expensive for most people until only 200 years ago.

Before a book can be printed, someone has to write it. Over the centuries, people have invented a host of different machines that make the job of writing easier. 150 years ago, the typewriter began to replace the pen. The office typewriter, in turn, has been gradually replaced by the desktop computer since the early 1980s.

The computer has had a bigger impact on the way people publish (put together and print) books than anything else since the invention of moveable type. Using the Internet, a global network of computers, people can publish work around the world without using a scrap of paper. In the future, the computer could be truly intelligent. The machine that helps you write and publish words may even help you to think.

FIRST WRITING

WORD PROCESSORS

When early writers made a mistake, they could wipe their page completely clean. That's because they wrote on tablets of wet clay. The clay didn't set until it was baked in the sun. The earliest clay tablets are over 5300 years old.

People today use word processors, special writing programs that run on computers, to edit pages easily as they go along.

MAKING YOUR MARK

The Ancient Chinese knew how to make inks that lasted. Their best inks are still legible 4000 years after they were used.

The main ingredient of these inks was charcoal, black stuff made from burnt wood. This was mixed with gum so it could be stored in a thick gooey state on the end of a stick. When ink was needed, writers dabbed these ink sticks in water to make a runny black liquid.

MAKING PAPER

PAPERMAKERS

The first paper was made when dinosaurs still roamed the Earth. Using dried wood mashed into a pulp, the earliest papermakers were wasps. These insects, who have always built their own nests from home-made paper, learnt the art of papermaking 300 million years before humans did. Humans discovered how to make paper a mere 2000 years ago. Modern paper was invented in China. Cai Lun of Lei-yang, one of the earliest papermakers, threw chopped-up fish nets, bark and plant fibres together to make sheets to write on. It took another 1000 years for Chinese papermaking know-how to travel from China to Europe, via the Arab world.

FORGET IT!
YOUR BRAIN'S
FAR TOO
SMALL TO
FIGURE IT OUT!

FIBRE PROVIDER

Plant fibre – paper's main ingredient – is so thin and light that a fibre long enough to stretch all the way around the Earth would weigh only fifteen kilogrammes. Plant fibre is also very strong. If you look at paper under the microscope, you'll see it's made up of a tangled web of plant fibres. This gives paper its strength. Plant fibre is made of 'cellulose' – a chemical that is also important in the film industry (see **Films to get your teeth into** *page 98*).

FROM RAGS TO RICHES

Hundreds of years ago, used clothing was the main ingredient of paper in Europe. Poor women and children would cut up rags to make paper for the rich. Once they had chopped rags into small pieces, they boiled them up with wood ash, then hit them many times until they turned into a slushy pulp. Lime, which was sometimes added to speed up pulping, gave paper a lovely, creamy colour. Rag paper was used to write on – and to make banknotes. Two hundred years ago, this anonymous poem summed up the paper trade:

RAGS MAKE PAPER
PAPER MAKES MONEY
MONEY MAKES BANKS
BANKS MAKE LOANS
LOANS MAKE BEGGARS
BEGGARS MAKE RAGS.

HELP

FANCY PATTERNS

People have known how to make watermarks almost as long as they have known how to make paper. Watermarks, the patterns you can see when you hold paper up to the light, are formed when pulp dries to form paper. Anything leaning on the drying pulp will leave its mark. The oldest watermarks were formed by bamboo covers that were put over drying pulp. Soon, people realised they could leave special marks on paper – giving paper its own special signature.

FORGING AHEAD

One banknote forger was so cunning, the secret of his work went with him to the grave. Set up in 1694, the Bank of England has seen a fair number of attempts to forge notes over its history. Some forgers, like the linen seller Richard William Vaughan who tried to write bigger numbers on his notes, were useless.

One, named John Mathieson, was a much better forger than most. When he was eventually caught in 1778, the bank couldn't work out how he'd made notes that were so realistic. The best thing about Mathieson's notes was his watermark. Mathieson, who explained he could paint the watermarks on to the paper, generously offered to reveal his methods if the bank would spare his life. Sadly for him, his offer was rejected and he was sentenced to death. Shortly after, the Bank of England gave their banknotes far more elaborate, curvy watermarks to make them much harder to copy.

LETHAL LINEN

Egyptian mummies were used to make paper during the American Civil War. Short of rags at home, some American paper manufacturers imported mummies, unwrapped them, then used their bindings to make pulp. Sadly, their scheme caused an epidemic among rag cutters as the mummies carried the deadly disease cholera. To make matters worse, some of the paper made from mummies was sold to butchers' shops. The butchers used it to wrap meat, spreading the epidemic even further.

HAVEN'T THEY HEARD OF THE CURSE OF THE MUMMY?

WASTE PAPER

On average, every person in the UK uses twice their own weight in paper a year. Paper is made automatically by huge paper mills that work around the clock. Every week, each mill makes enough paper to stretch from London to New York. Almost half the paper we buy is used to make newspapers, books, magazines and leaflets. Some of it is made from recycled paper (paper that is made from mashed-up old paper) but the rest comes from freshly-chopped forests that have been grown specially for paper-making. Half the paper we use ends up buried in giant holes in the ground called 'landfill sites'. Until recently, scientists thought paper and other rubbish would rot inside these sites, as though the sites were giant compost heaps. If the paper rotted, it would end up as useful waste materials and would release a gas called carbon dioxide that would help more trees to grow. Astonishingly though, archaeologists digging into old dumps have found that buried paper hardly rots at all, even over 50 years or more. So it looks like hardly any paper we bury in dumps will ever make paper again.

IN PRINT

WISE MOVE

Between about 1450 and 1500, people in Europe were able to print more books than they had in the last 1000 years. That's because moveable type was introduced. Moveable type is a set of separate little printing blocks, each with a raised part in the shape of a back-to-front number or letter. Moveable type can be lined up quickly and easily to make a printed page. Once the letters have been arranged, they can be used to make any number of copies of a page. Before moveable type came along, books had to be written by hand. This was a slow and expensive business. Handwritten books cost so much, only monasteries, colleges and very rich people could afford to buy them. Moveable type eventually made books cheap enough for ordinary people to afford. This meant millions could learn to read for the first time ever.

PRINTER'S PROBLEM

The saying 'mind your ps and qs' probably comes from the printing trade. Printers used to have to set up letters back-to-front on their presses. If they were working fast, they sometimes got their letters muddled. For instance, they may have mixed up the letters p and q. Printers in English only have 26 letters to worry about, but the Chinese have many thousands. As early as 1297, a Chinese printer, Wang Zhen, made a set of 6000 wooden printing blocks. Every block was for a different Chinese word. Almost 200 years before that, another Chinese printer, Bi Sheng, made blocks of letters out of clay. This was one of the earliest ever forms of moveable type.

TYPEWRITERS

TYPEWRITER TERROR

When the Abbé Clement proudly showed off his new invention, the typewriter, in 1855, his boss was far from impressed. The Count D'Aunay warned him that the typewriter could be used by anyone in their homeland, France, to make their own leaflets and pamphlets. It would be an easy way to spread rudeness or naughty ideas. The naughtiest of these was rebellion (fighting against the people who ran the country).

A TYPEWRITER? NEVER!

WHAT IF IT FELL IN THE WRONG HANDS?

HAND WRITING

To type a letter with the Cary Writing Glove, you simply had to roll your hand over the page. Nothing more than a pair of rubber gloves, the outside of Cary Writing Glove was covered in raised letters that you could cover in ink then press against a sheet of paper. Each glove contained a different set of letters. Useful words and letter groups like 'and', 'the', 'ing' and 'tion' were located on the thumbs. Sold in the 1890s, the Writing Glove was the craziest of a bunch of early typewriters – all of which hoped to become the next big thing.

PRINTING ERROR

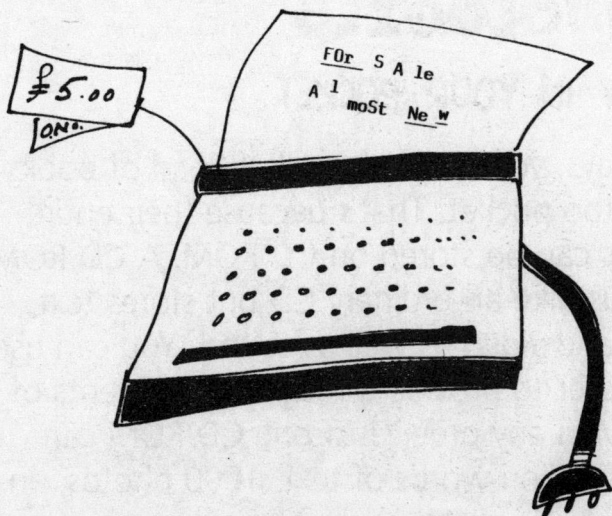

£5.00

ono.

FOr   S A le
A l moSt   Ne w

'The electric typewriter would eliminate to a greater extent the human element, and for that reason it is not likely to become popular.' When Charles Oden wrote this in 1917, he felt that people wouldn't like using a typewriter because it wasn't like a person. We now know he couldn't have been more wrong. Over the twentieth century, electric typewriters have transformed the office, letting people bash out words more easily than ever before. Since the early 1980s, they have been widely replaced by something that does even more things in the place of humans: the desktop computer.

NEW PUBLISHING TECHNOLOGIES

LIBRARY IN YOUR POCKET

These days, you can carry a shelf load of books in your top pocket. That's because their entire contents can be stored on CD ROM. A CD ROM works just like an ordinary CD but stores text, images and video as well as sound. You can use a computer to browse through the contents of a CD ROM in any order. Just one CD ROM can hold 30 million words of text, 1000 photos, an hour of music or 30 minutes of video.

ENCYCLOPEDIA BRITANNICA

I LIKE TO TRAVEL LIGHT

HOME WORK

It's now possible to show your work to people around the world without having to pay a penny in printing costs. That's because you can put things on the 'world wide web' – a vast collection of documents that you can look up on the Internet (*see* **Web of war** *page 34*). Anyone who can get on to the Internet can look at your work if you put it there. There are lots of good reasons to put your work on the Internet. It brings your work to millions, it costs very little and it can include pictures, sound and videos. You can also put special words or pictures into your work, called 'hyperlinks'. People can click on these to whisk themselves to other parts of your work or to other people's information. Putting work on the web does have a few disadvantages. Unless people print it out, they only see your work on a screen. What's more, anyone who's rude enough can easily copy the work you have written and steal your ideas.

A PAPERLESS SOCIETY?

As telephones, computers and the Internet become more widespread, some people have predicted we'll stop using paper altogether. Companies like Rank Xerox have experimented with 'paperless desks'. These shine pictures of notepads and books on to your desk from a special type of video projector controlled by a computer. Most of this is 'cutting edge' research – a paperless society is still a long way off. Although sales of computers and modems go up all the time (*see* **Global village** *page 33*), sales of newspapers and books don't go down. In fact, our use of paper increases every year. It seems that people like to look at information on computers – but they prefer snuggling up to a real book at bedtime.

WELL- YOU CAN'T SNUGGLE UP TO A CD ROM. CAN YOU....

COMPUTERS

SPACE FILLER

It's easy to talk to computers these days – but in 1969, the computer that did the calculations to get people to the Moon was very difficult to use. With no friendly computer screen, you had to communicate with it by punching holes in a sheet of card. That computer, which took up as much room as several chest freezers, had less memory than today's average mobile phone. That's because it was built before the days of microchips, tiny devices that squeeze millions of

electrical parts into a tiny space (*see* **Tiny trannies** *page 60*). Using microchips, engineers have been able to build computers that do very complicated things but can sit on a desktop. Almost all desktop computers today can draw easy-to-follow words and pictures on a video screen. They change these pictures when you use a keyboard or click a small computer control called a 'mouse'. These words and pictures that we take for granted today have been widely available only since the early 1980s.

WISHFUL THINKING?

The average desktop computer has roughly the same processing power as a snail. In other words, it can hold roughly the same amount of information and it shuffles that information around at roughly the same speed. On this scale of things, humans are way ahead of computers. But some scientists have predicted the most powerful computers around – 'supercomputers' – will have the same processing power as us by the year 2010. They've even forecast that ordinary desktop computers will be as brainy as us by the year 2030!

DOESN'T ADD UP

Always be wary of predictions about computers – after all, even T.J. Watson, the founder of computer giant IBM, is famous for getting one forecast wildly wrong. When he was asked earlier this century how many computers he expected to sell worldwide, he suggested five. Today, over 34 million desktop computers are sold around the world every year.

INTELLIGENCE TEST

If a computer has as much processing power as a human, will it be intelligent? In the 1950s, the computer pioneer Alan Turing suggested a simple way to test this. Hide a human and a computer behind a screen and ask them both some questions. The questions can be about anything at all. If you can't tell which answers come from the human and which come from the machine then your computer is truly intelligent. Although some computers can get by answering questions on a single subject, like Star Trek, no computer built so far has a hope of passing a proper 'Turing Test'. In fact, some computer programmers think this is so difficult to do, they should be looking at new ways to test a computer's intelligence.

CHAMPION GETS THE BLUES

When chess champion Garry Kasparov lost a match in 1997, he didn't take defeat very well. That's because he hadn't been beaten by a rival player – but by a computer. The computer in question, Deep Blue, was the first to outdo a chess champion. Using specially-written programmes, it studied Kasparov's playing style so it could find ways to fox him. Although the computer was the victor, it didn't have any of Kasparov's inspired thinking. Instead, it used its enormous memory laboriously to think through thousands of possible moves until it found the way to get the best results.

COMPUTERS WITH ATTITUDE

When someone turned off a new type of computer program, one tiny part at a time, its life seemed to flash before it. In other words, its memory seemed to fire randomly until it ran out of power. Although very primitive, this program, called a 'neural network', was made of thousands of separate 'cells'. These cells could send messages to each other just like the cells in a human brain. Scientists have been experimenting with neural networks in the hope they will shed light on the ways we think – and produce more intelligent machines. Neural networks have been shown to learn, evolve and even get angry – just like us.

Quiz

1 The earliest writing was on
   a) bark
   b) tablets of clay
   c) cave walls

2 The first ever paper was made
   a) when dinosaurs roamed the Earth
   b) when the Chinese invented gunpowder
   c) when Romans invaded Britain

3 Cellulose has been used to make
   a) film
   b) paper
   c) false teeth

4 During the American Civil war, people made paper from
   a) banknotes
   b) mummies
   c) fish skin

5 The Count D'Aunay didn't like the typewriter because he thought it
   would spread
   a) disease
   b) rebellion
   c) the German language

6 The average desktop computer has roughly the same processing power as
a) a cat
b) a chimpanzee
c) a snail

7 Deep Blue is
a) a remote-controlled submarine
b) a chess computer
c) a communications satellite

8 Half the paper we use ends up
a) littering the streets
b) buried underground
c) in the sewers

9 The Cary Writing Glove is a
a) novelty typewriter
b) glove to stop writers' cramp
c) secret society of US writers

10 Lime makes paper
a) wrinkly in texture
b) easier to fold
c) creamy in colour

CHAPTER 4

In the picture

Nothing records events in our lives better than our photograph albums. Most people's albums are brimming with snaps of births, weddings, holidays and other special events that can tell others a great deal about their past.

The Victorians were the first people to experience the thrill of capturing their image on a photograph. They were also the first to come across one of its drawbacks. A simple photograph, unlike a painting, cannot lie about the way someone really looks. These days, this isn't such a problem. A skilled person called a 'graphic artist' can 'touch-up' a photograph to flatter a subject as skilfully as any portrait painter.

Photography has enabled us to experienced the thrill of watching a movie. Films use a stream of thousands of photographs to create moving pictures. Millions of us are entertained every year by make-believe worlds on film. Soon, technologies like virtual reality and the interactive movie may enable us to step into these worlds and change what goes on in them. When this happens, we will become part of living, changing photographs.

EARLY CAMERAS

IN THE DARK

The earliest cameras were the size of a small room. First used by the Ancient Greeks – centuries before photography was invented – these walk-in, darkened boxes had one small pinhole to let in light. Light outside would pour through the pinhole and shine on to the back wall, forming an image. Artists like Leonardo da Vinci used these rooms, called 'camera obscuras'. They traced around the images made on the back wall to learn how to draw life-like pictures. 'Camera obscura' means 'darkened room' – it's also the origin of the word 'camera'.

NEGATIVE THINKING

A young man called William Henry Fox Talbot was inspired to make the first photographic negative because he wasn't very good at drawing. In 1833, Fox Talbot had taken a mini camera obscura on holiday in Italy but was fed up with the poor quality of his terrible tracings. He wanted to find a way to fix the image made by the rays of light inside his box. He went home and experimented with chemicals called 'silver salts'. One day, after leaving a paste of silver salts on a glass plate inside his camera, he came back to find a negative image of the room around him. Although it was far less exposed (in other words, far darker) than a negative today, it did show the main window of the room – the library at Lacock Abbey. It showed this well enough to count how many panes of glass it had.

INSTANT CAMERA?

KEEP SMILING, CHILDREN...

There was no such thing as a quick snap in the 1840s. The most popular type of photograph at that time was a daguerreotype – an image made in a sheet of copper that had a thin coating of silver. Depending on the brightness of the weather, you had to sit completely still for anything up to fifteen minutes while your daguerreotype was taken. As any movements made a blurred photograph, your head was fixed in a clamp. This meant photography was a very starchy affair. In the 1850s, new ways to make photographs like the 'collodion process' came along that could take an image in just a few seconds. This allowed a few pioneering photographers, like Julia Margaret Cameron, to create portraits with a far more natural look. These days, the fastest cameras take snaps in less than a millionth of a second.

PHOTOGRAPHY BOOM

'The sixpenny photograph is doing more for the poor than all the philanthropists in the world.' This was someone's view of photography at the height of its boom in the 1850s. Photographs were so fashionable and affordable, almost 3000 photographic studios sprang up in London. A town in the US named itself

Daguerreville and started producing over three million daguerreotype plates a year. Over the next 30 years, people even started putting their photos on visiting cards. People would produce different photos for different occasions – ones with them wearing gloves for formal visits, ones with them carrying an umbrella for rainy days.

FRUITY THOUGHTS

Rather than cheese, you were advised to think of prunes when you had your daguerreotype taken in the 1840s. When you mouthed this word, it gave your face a suitably dignified

expression while you waited for your picture to be taken. You were advised not to wear violet or pure white. These colours reflected so much light, they left ugly blank patches on the finished picture.

STARS IN THEIR EYES

The visiting card craze gave people their first opportunities to see real mug shots of the rich and famous. When a studio put a new photo of a celebrity in the window, people flocked to buy copies of it. People enjoyed collecting pictures of prime ministers and royals as well as actors, entertainers and infamous criminals.

CAMERA NEVER LIES

When asked by Queen Victoria if he felt his trade was threatened by photography, a famous portrait artist replied, 'Ah no Madame. Photography cannot flatter!' In the 1880s, everyone wanted to satisfy their vanity by having their photographs taken. However, unlike the portrait artist, there was a limit to what a photographer could do to improve on what nature had created.

PRETTY! ANYONE I KNOW?

PAINTING IN THE CLOUDS

When snapshot cameras became popular in the late 1880s, you could buy your own sky to add on to your photographs. Real blue skies looked awful in early snapshots. As film was over-sensitive to blue, skies came out pitch black on the negative. This meant they looked incredibly bright on the final photograph (dark areas on a negative come out light on the photograph they make). From the 1850s, people got round this by painting their own sky in on the negative. If they made this grey-black, it would come out grey-white on the photograph. Some people

added their own clouds – they painted them on to their negatives with black, Indian ink. By the 1880s, photographers started selling ready-made skies, complete with clouds, that you could add to a negative to get just the right look.

SNAPS AT A SNIP

It cost two weeks' wages to have a film developed in the 1880s. Most people didn't earn enough money in an entire month to buy a snapshot camera. In 1888, an American George Eastman pioneered easy photography for all. Supplying snapshot cameras and a developing service, he had the slogan 'You press the button, we do the rest'.

Most people couldn't afford to make use of his service until the cheap and cheerful Brownie camera appeared in 1900. A fraction of the cost of earlier cameras, one hundred thousand Brownies were sold in less than a year. When these appeared, lots of people could afford to take their own snaps for the first time ever.

COLOUR IMAGES

POTATO PHOTOS

We have to thank the humble potato for the first colour photographs. Introduced in 1904, the Autochrome process used grains of potato starch sandwiched between the light-sensitive chemicals and the glass backing plate. Autochrome was invented by the Lumière brothers, two men who were also pioneers of the cinema (*see* **What a scream** *page 100*). As the grains were painted different colours, they acted as filters, only letting some colours of light pass through them. If you held an Autochrome picture up to the light, you could see it in colour.

FIRST MOVING PICTURES

TRICKS OF THE FLICKS

Films work because they trick our eyes. We see images when light falls on to the back of our eyes – but there's a limit to how fast our eyes can notice changes in the light that reaches them. If the images in front of our eyes change faster than about sixteen times a second, our brain fills in the gaps between the pictures and sees them as a single, moving image. Films show a stream of photos that change about twenty times a second – fast enough for this to happen.

MOVING PICTURES COINED

In the 1820s, the English scientist John Herschel bet a friend he could make the head and tail of a coin show at the same time. To the amazement of his friend, when he spun the coin really fast, images of the head and tail merged together. Using a simple trick of the eyes, he had won the bet. Tricks like this were very fashionable around that time and many toys were sold that made use of them.

GAMBLING HORSES

It was a far more expensive experiment that led to another important discovery about motion pictures – that they can be made from a sequence of still photographs. In 1872, Leland Stanford, a keen racehorse breeder, hired a photographer Eadweard Muybridge to help him win a bet. Stanford had bet a friend that at some point when a horse runs, it takes all four feet off the ground at once. Some people says Stanford made a 'sportsman's bet' – he didn't bet any money – others say he bet no less than $25,000. Stanford certainly would have been able to afford such a gamble. A multimillionaire, Stanford was one of the richest men in America.

LONG STRUGGLE

It took Muybridge five years of research to come up with the ultimate way to settle Stanford's bet. In the final year, Muybridge set up a row of twelve cameras along a racetrack and tied a string to each one. As it galloped past each camera, the horse triggered the camera's shutter, taking a photo. Muybridge showed his pictures to the delighted Stanford to prove that the horse did take all feet off the ground when it ran. He also put his photos into a simple toy, the Phenakistoscope. When he spun the Phenakistoscope, he could see the galloping horse as a moving picture. Muybridge's experiment, which enabled Stanford to win his bet, cost no less than $100,000 to complete. Fortunately, as Stanford was incredibly wealthy, he had no problems finding this much cash.

FIRST FILM SHOOT

Étienne-Jules Marey really did 'shoot' the first motion picture – his early camera was based on an automatic pistol. Instead of a string of bullets, Marey's gun contained a glass plate covered with light-sensitive chemicals.

When Marey triggered his 'photographic gun' it took lots of photos very quickly, one after the other. All the photos ended up on the same plate. Marey used them to help people to see how things move. In 1888, Marey replaced his glass plate with a roll of paper film. He could use this to take far more pictures at a time.

Marey was a physiologist, someone who studies the way the body works, so he took lots of films of animals and people in action. Using his gun, he could take photos amazingly fast – only one 6000th of a second apart. This allowed him to photograph actions that happened far too fast for the eye to see.

FIRST MOVIE FILM

FILMS TO GET YOUR TEETH INTO

It was a new material for making false teeth that paved the way for modern film. In 1862, Alexander Parkes patented this new material: celluloid (you can find out what a patent is in **A close call** *page 25*). A type of plastic, celluloid is made from cellulose – the stringy fibre that gives plants their strength. You can read about an entirely different use of cellulose in **Fibre provider** *page 67*.

If celluloid was mixed with white powder, it made an excellent substitute for ivory. It was used to make everything from dentures and billiard balls to shirt collars and pistons. In 1884, an American inventor, George Eastman, found that celluloid, which is light sensitive, also made an excellent photographic film.

ROTTEN MOVIES

Every day, experts are working as fast as they can to save thousands of national treasures from destruction. Around the world, there are millions of metres of early films that are printed on celluloid. Even when they are sitting in steel cans, these films are all slowly decaying. Heat or light makes them rot even faster. Places like the British Film Institute, London, have film archives. These are places that try to keep copies of old films in good condition so people can enjoy them in years to come. Every year, they copy old celluloid films on to modern plastic ones. Although modern films last longer than celluloid, even they are unlikely to last forever.

SNIFFY ABOUT MOVIES

The American inventor Thomas Edison put together the first movie film. Interestingly though, he only saw film as a nice accompaniment to his other big invention: the phonograph (*see* **Music to their ears?** *page 46*). In the 1880s, Edison was successful enough to employ a workshop full of people to help him develop his ideas. He asked some of them to find a way to etch tiny photos on to a disk so moving pictures could be recorded just like sound. Aware of Eastman's work, one of his staff suggested Edison tried using celluloid instead. In 1890, Edison made the first celluloid film – a short movie showing one of his staff sneezing.

THROUGH THE PEEPHOLE

Edison's early moving pictures could hardly be called 'big screen entertainment'. Rather than projecting his films, Edison designed a special booth, called a Kinetoscope, that allowed one person to view them at a time. Each film, which lasted up to half a minute, whizzed past a tiny peephole viewer at a rate of 40 frames per second. To keep his films running smoothly through a Kinetoscope, Edison put a string of holes on each side of them so they would slip neatly over a set a teeth. Films have holes like this to this day. In the 1890s, thousands of Kinetoscopes were placed all over America. Millions of people put a coin in a slot to see their first-ever movie.

WHAT A SCREAM!

Audiences shrieked and ducked out of the way when they saw a train coming towards them on one of the first big screen movies. The film, about a train arriving in a station, was first screened for the paying public in 1895. It was put together by the brothers Auguste and Louis Lumière. After playing with Edison's Kinetoscope, they decided to make their own films and project them on to a big screen for a much bolder effect. The Lumière brothers let audiences watch a film together on a big screen for the first time ever – they really were the pioneers of cinema. Once Edison saw the success of the Lumière brothers' big screen entertainment, he decided to make his own film projector, the Vitascope.

MYSTERY MAN

One of the most important breakthroughs in cinema was made by a man whose life story is worthy of any film thriller. That man was the French experimenter Louis Le Prince who lived and worked in Leeds, UK. In 1888, Le Prince made an all-in-one film camera and projector that worked in a whole new way. Instead of moving film continuously, it switched between frames rapidly, but paused on each one. His 'intermittent' film looked smoother than any others, even when it played as slow as sixteen frames per second. In the 1890s, the Lumière brothers also used intermittent film. This meant their pictures looked much smoother than Edison's. Although he was a pioneer, Le Prince never benefited from his breakthrough. In 1890, he mysteriously disappeared from a moving train, never to be seen again.

COLOUR FILM

PAINTING A PICTURE

SOME OF US WILL DO ANYTHING TO GET INTO THE MOVIES!

FILM

Before people worked out how to make colour movies, films were coloured the hard way. Film makers used cheap labour to colour every frame of their film by hand. A typical early film, such as Edison's *Annabell's Butterfly* would be about fifteen metres long. Young women would be employed to paint fine colour on to every one of its 700 frames. Each one would be responsible for painting in one particular colour. As they were paid so badly, a hand-coloured film in 1902 was only about 14 shillings (70 pence) more expensive than a black and white one. Hand-colouring enabled coloured film to be seen just a few years after the first-ever movies.

HINT OF A TINT

In the 1920s, most films were spiced up by adding a dash of Inferno, Nocturne or Firelight. These were all tints that could be painted on a film to add to the drama. Films in the 1920s were far too long to colour in by hand. Tints offered a cheaper alternative, giving key parts of the film a special coloured glow. Inferno, for example, was used in fire scenes – it tinted the film shocking red. By the 1920s, tints were so popular, pure black and white films were a rarity.

REMOTE CONTROL

Around 1910, some cinemas could only show genuine colour films if the projectionist could talk on the telephone to someone in the audience. That's because the earliest colour film processes, like Kinemacolor and Chromochrome, created colour images by playing more than one film at once. As each film was a different colour, the combined films created a coloured image. Unfortunately, the films often drifted apart or got out of step, creating a fuzzy, badly-coloured mess. When some projectionists ran a Chromochrome film, they used a telephone to keep in touch with someone in the audience. As soon as the colours went adrift, the person in the audience would let them know. They could put the film right before it got too messy.

BLONDE BOMBSHELL

When the colour film process Technicolor appeared in 1922, audiences could enjoy a whole rainbow of glorious colours – well, any colour except blue. Today, Technicolor is very good at showing all colours. But until the mid-1930s, Technicolor was lousy at blue. That's because it made its picture by adding together two separate colour films: one red and one green. This early Technicolor was also pretty useless at showing blonde hair – which is why one Hollywood film maker made the surprising comment that 'platinum blonde was out'. Although early Technicolor had its drawbacks, Hollywood did experiment with it. Next time there's a musical from the 1920s or early 1930s on the television, take a look at it. Although the film is in black and white, it's bound to include a short Technicolor spectacular somewhere near the end – and this won't have a hint of blue.

DOTTY SYSTEM

Next time you watch a film, look out for little dots that appear in the corner of the screen every now and then. These dots, called 'academy marks', tell the projectionist when to put on the next reel of film. Feature films tend to last about 90 minutes, but reels get too bulky if they're more than 30 minutes long. So films tend to be made up of three or more reels. One academy mark appears when it's time to get the next reel ready. Another one appears when it's time to switch reels. In state-of-the-art cinemas, a projectionist can splice together reels to make one big film. In older ones, the projectionist has to be ready to put on a new reel before the old one runs out.

COMPUTERS AND FILM

DIGITAL FILMS

These days, films with special effects are still put together frame by frame. In a process that's far more painstaking than any hand-colouring of the early 1900s, big film companies employ computer graphics experts to make imaginary worlds come to life. A computerised effect

called 'morphing', for example, lets them melt one object seamlessly into another. Another, called 'ray tracing', lets them create realistic reflections in shiny, imaginary objects. Unlike the unfortunate women who hand-painted early films, special-effects people are paid handsomely for their work. That's why blockbuster films cost anything up to a billion dollars to make.

CHANGE OF SCENE

These days, film makers just need to press a few buttons to remove unwanted objects from movies – a phone box in a film about the Romans for example. They also have a host of other special effects they can use to add drama to a background scene. Using a new branch of mathematics, called 'fractal geometry', they can make realistic clouds, mountains and rocks using nothing but numbers. Compare this to the early photographers who used to paint in skies on their negatives (*see* **Painting in the clouds** *page 92*). Fractal geometry is most often used in computer games to make realistic, moving landscapes that can change quickly and that take up very little computer memory.

PUTTING ON A FRONT

You may not think that TV weather presenters make the best actors, but they're using their acting skills all the time. We see a weather presenter standing in front of a large map of the country, moving effortlessly from tonight's weather to tomorrow's. However, in reality, the presenter is standing in front a plain wall. The presenter has to remember where the map will appear on your screens and act as though it's really there. A computer adds the map into the background of the picture before it reaches your screen.

FUZZY THINKING

Usually, we think computers can tell us the right way to do something – but recently, scientists have made computers think in an altogether less logical, fuzzier way. Using a way of thinking called 'fuzzy logic', computers can be used to make sense of problems that aren't cut and dried. A computer program that uses fuzzy logic doesn't decide whether something is true or false. Instead, it thinks in terms of 'absolutely correct', 'probably true', 'not altogether out of the question' and 'mmm ... I don't think so'. In fact, it weighs up problems very much like we

do. Fuzzy logic can be used to clean up faded, blurred and scratched old films. Recently, it was also used to sharpen blurred images from the Hubble Space Telescope (see **History lesson** *page 136*). The images were blurred because the telescope's giant lens was faulty.

DIGITAL PHOTOGRAPHS

Some modern cameras don't need film at all. That's because they take pictures digitally (*see* **Done with numbers** *page 22*). A grid of sensors inside the digital camera takes a snapshot of the scene. The camera stores the snapshot as lots of numbers. These numbers say how the colour and brightness of the picture vary from sensor to sensor. This snapshot can be kept in the camera and saved at a later date on to a computer. Digital cameras take pictures that look very coarse and speckly at the moment but they are improving every year. One day they may be so good, photographic film will seem as outdated as the original daguerreotypes.

PONG IN THE HOME

In the early 1970s, a game with the simple rules 'avoid missing ball for high score' changed people's views of moving pictures for ever. That game was the TV tennis match called Pong. A forerunner of 'console games' like SuperMario, Pong was a revelation to millions. It gave them their first chance to interact (play) with images on a screen. We now take computer games for granted. Interactive images (pictures we can control and change) are becoming part of our everyday lives. In a recent survey, more American children had heard of the computer game character SuperMario than the Disney hero Mickey Mouse.

LOSING THE PLOT

When you watch the movie *Burncycle*, you can make up the plot. That's because it's an 'interactive movie' – a show that lets the viewers decide what different characters should do. So far, interactive movies are still in their infancy. They tend to be only a few minutes long and they can only be played on computers. Keep an eye out for them though – as computing technology improves, interactive movies are set to get better and better. Soon, we could all be enjoying interactive movies on a TV that's been souped-up by a 'set top box' (*see* **Tailoring the telly** *page 132*). Using the Internet, it's already possible to play computer games with people who are thousands of kilometres away. At the moment, the Internet works too slowly to let people share games that have fast-moving pictures. But if the Internet gets faster, it may one day be possible to share an interactive movie with someone in another part of the world.

VIRTUAL MOVIES

It's already possible to step into movies, as well as watch them. A technology called 'virtual reality' (VR) allows us to do this. VR lets you totally immerse yourself in a movie – it gives you the sensation of walking around it, listening and even touching the events around you. At the moment, the only VR films around are simple movies of landscapes and buildings. Computing technology will have to advance a long way before we can start making VR films that have realistic characters and complex storylines. When we get to that stage, our early experiences of VR may seem as silly as the experiences of the people in the Lumière theatre who ducked when they saw a train coming.

THAT SUITS ME JUST FINE....

Quiz

1 People used camera obscuras to
   a) hide their cameras
   b) draw pictures
   c) develop films

2 In the 1860s, there was a craze for putting personal photographs on
   a) visiting cards
   b) dogs collars
   c) shoe leathers

3 When having your photo taken in the 1880s you were advised to say
   a) cheese
   b) fork
   c) prunes

4 The first colour snaps were made possible by
   a) the potato
   b) the banana
   c) the brussel sprout

5 Projectionists change the reel of a feature film when
   a) a little dot appears on the screen
   b) actors say a code word
   c) lights flicker in the theatre

6 Fuzzy logic has been used to
   a) select lottery balls
   b) steer satellites
   c) sharpen blurred photographs

7 Etienne-Jules Marey made a movie camera from
   a) a spinning top
   b) an automatic pistol
   c) a sewing machine

8 Early Technicolor wasn't very good at shooting
   a) blondes
   b) stripes
   c) close-ups

9 The rules for the simple video game Pong were
   a) defend Earth from invaders from Pong
   b) catch the skunk for maximum points
   c) avoid missing ball for high score

10 Pop star Kyoto Date is unusual because she is
   a) a talking horse
   b) made by computer
   c) only available on video

CHAPTER 5

Spreading the news

How did you hear about the release of Nelson Mandela from prison or the death of Diana, Princess of Wales? Unless you were told about these events by someone you know, you probably found out about them by watching TV, listening to the radio or reading the newspaper.

Vast, highly organised news networks enable important stories to reach every major newsdesk of the world in minutes. If you watch the TV news, you'll hear reports of events that happened less than an hour before. If you see a 'live' satellite broadcast, you'll be able to witness news events on the other side of the world almost as they happen.

Without TV, radio and newspapers, we'd find it hard to know what's going on in the world. But no programme or paper has the time or space to tell you everything that's news. A headline in one country may barely make the news in another.

The people who own and run the news services have a big say in what we will get to know about. This means they can have a huge influence on what we think — and even how we vote at an election. It's no wonder then that governments keep a close eye on what appears on the news — and on who puts the news together.

NEWSPAPERS

ROYAL RAG

The longest
running
newspaper
kept going for
1292 years.
This paper
also had one
of the smallest
circulations –
just a few

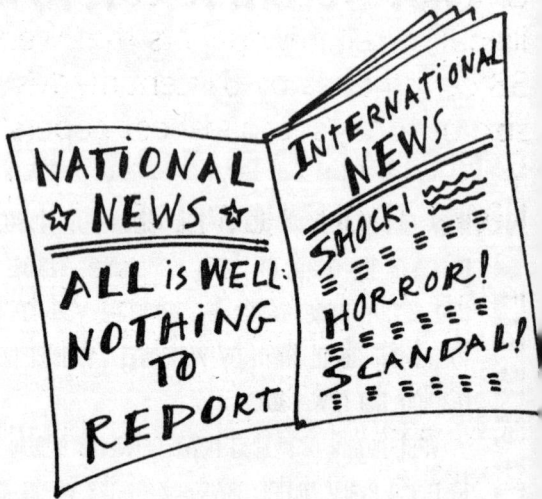

dozen copies of each issue were printed. The
paper was written to keep people up to date
with news in the Chinese court.

BIG PAPERS GET THE CHOP

Hundreds of years ago, newspapers in the UK
only reported foreign news. That's because the
editors were wary about upsetting the
government and ending up in prison. The
longest-running paper with a large circulation is
The Times. Started in 1785, this paper was first
called *The Daily Universal Register*. James Walter
and his son were inspired to make it after they
found a printing press that could print 5000

copies of a page an hour. In the eighteenth century, Parliament passed a law making it illegal to sell newspapers that were bigger than 38 centimetres by 61 centimetres in size – the size of today's 'broadsheet papers'.

NEWS FROM NOWHERE

In the 1850s, *The Times* had to pay twice as much as other newspapers for its articles. That's because it refused to print the name of the news agency, Reuters, who had supplied the stories.

Paul Julius Reuter set up his organisation in 1850 as a cheap way for papers to report the news. Without Reuters, a paper could only keep up to date with world news if it could afford to put a journalist in every major country.

After the development of the electric telegraph system (*see* **The electric telegraph** *page 15-19*), Reuters was able to offer a truly international service. These days, Reuters is available 'on-line' to any paying subscribers and can send a news flash around the world in seconds.

BEFORE TELEVISION

SEEING THE LIGHT

The pioneers of television are in debt to a young engineer who left some telegraph cables too close to a window (you can find out what a telegraph is in **The electric telegraph** *page 15-19*). One sunny day in 1879, Joseph May told his supervisor that he'd noticed something strange about the telegraph cables he'd been checking. The ones that had been left out in the light allowed electricity to pass through them more easily than ones that were fresh out of the box. The cables were made of selenium, a metal we now know is sensitive to light. Fascinated by this discovery, the company's chief electrician, Willoughby Smith, wrote a note about it to the Society of Telegraph Engineers.

Smith's letter, which conveniently forgot to mention May's involvement with the discovery, triggered a spark of inventions, all claiming to 'see by radio.'

HA HA HA

FIRST BUT NOT FOREMOST

Pile ointments, marmalade, rustless razors and footwarmers were just a few of the things that John Logie Baird tried to invent before he had a go at television. Many books will tell you that John Logie Baird invented television – but this isn't strictly true. In fact, if Baird had been luckier with his earlier ventures, he may not have dabbled with television at all. All his life, Baird had been desperate to invent something that would make him rich. After his pile cream made him itchy, his marmalade company failed and he cut himself on his rustless razor, he decided that television was his best option.

JUNK TV

A hatbox, a pair of scissors, some darning needles and bicycle lamp lenses – just some of the junk that made Baird's first television. Baird had read a patent written by a young engineer Paul Nipkow (you can find out what a patent is in **A close call** *page 25*).

Written in 1883, his patent showed a picture of a disk that was full of holes arranged in a spiral. Nipkow suggested you could spin two of these disks together, one in front of each other, to peek at the scene behind it bit by bit. We now call this 'scanning' the scene. Baird used two Nipkow disks and put a sheet of the light-sensitive material selenium behind them to pick out the light from each part of the scene (*see* **Seeing the light** *page 118*). The selenium let electricity pass through it more easily when the brightness of each part of the scene increased. Baird used the current running through the selenium to control another machine that also used Nipkow disks. This second machine showed an exact copy of the scene.

FIRST TV PICTURE

Baird, the first person to put Nipkow's ideas to work, managed to get the first-ever TV picture in 1923. Some people say the first picture he made was a crude image of a cross – others say it was someone's hand. Whatever the picture was, Baird managed to send this flickering image by television from one room of his lodgings to another. After Baird publicised his breakthrough, he had plenty of visitors – until his landlord got wise to his experiments and threw him out.

TRICK CAMERA

When Baird showed people his television pictures, some of them thought he was playing a trick on them. One engineer, invited to Baird's new lodgings in 1925, tricked Baird out of the room for a moment. When Baird returned, he found him scrambling on the floor, looking for hidden mirrors. Although the public were impressed with Baird's efforts, the BBC was not. Until they were forced to by law, they refused to let him broadcast television from their studios. They felt he was misleading the public about the quality of his ropy images.

RUBBISH.

T.V.

BBC

DEAD END

The televisions we use today aren't really anything like Baird's early system. They came from a completely different design, first suggested by the American engineer A.A. Campbell Swinton in 1908. Swinton's system made a picture by firing a stream of tiny particles, called electrons, at a screen. A system just like it was developed by the electronics company Marconi EMI in the 1920s. In 1936, the British government asked the BBC to try out this system, along with Baird's, on a regular basis from their studios in Alexandra Palace, London.

LINE BY LINE

If you could slow down your television set, you would see the clever way it makes a picture on the screen. Your television picture is made of about 600 separate horizontal lines. In a split second, a beam zigzags down the entire screen. It moves right to left, then flies back from left to right, changing direction hundreds of times as it moves from the top to the bottom of the screen. The beam is made of billions of tiny particles called 'electrons' and the screen is covered in a material that is sensitive to these. When the electrons hit any part of the screen, they make it glow.

The beam is only about half a millimetre wide so it only lights up a tiny part of the screen at a time. However, as it zigzags down the screen very fast, it only takes a 25th of a second to light up the whole screen. Our brains merge all the glowing parts of the screen together to see a complete picture (*see* **Tricks of the flicks** *page 94 to find out why*). Although our screen has about 600 lines, Baird's first television produced a picture using only 30. These lines were drawn vertically to make a very poor quality picture.

BETWEEN THE LINES

Most TV broadcasts have bonus information that's tucked into unused lines at the top of the picture. Although most modern TV pictures are made up of about 600 lines (see **Line by line** *page 123*), up to 60 of these lines may be tucked out of sight at the top or bottom of the screen. TV companies often send extra information in these unused lines. Some TVs have equipment to turn this bonus information into text. This service, called Teletext, gives you news, weather and other useful information. When more of us have 'set top boxes' that will give us interactive TV (see **Tailoring the telly** *page 132*), Teletext may soon start looking out of date. For the time being though, it's a very handy service – and one of the quickest ways to find out what's on the telly.

CRYSTAL CLEAR

Soon, some TV companies may have to chuck out most of their old props. That's because their TV picture may be about to improve so much, the crude props they use today will look lousy. Today's TV picture is made up of about 600 separate horizontal lines (see **Line by line** *page 123*) but some TV companies are planning to make pictures that use 1000. The new system, called High Definition Television (HDTV), may be broadcast very soon by a few TV companies. No one knows if HDTV will catch on. After all, it will cost lots of money to make HDTV programmes and people who want to see them in their full glory will need to buy a new HDTV set. Some people have said that HDTV is far less certain to happen than widescreen TV (TV shows with a wide picture). However, some experimental HDTV programmes have already been made. We will be able to watch HDTV programmes on our ordinary TV sets – although, of course, we'll miss out on all the extra detail.

HANG ON!
YOU STILL CAN
SEE HDTV
PROGRAMMES
ON YOUR
OLD SETS!

WHAT A PICTURE!

Gaudy make-up was a must for the first TV presenters, even though early television was in black and white. In the Alexandra Palace studios in 1930s, the BBC used to swap between studios every day – one day, they'd be in the Baird studio, the next day they'd be in the studio full of Marconi EMI equipment. The crew always preferred to work in the Marconi EMI studio as Baird's was a hot and dangerous place to be. It had bright lights, huge heavy cameras and open tanks of toxic chemicals. The picture quality on Baird's system was so poor, presenters could only be seen if they painted their faces yellow and put thick blue lines around their lips and eyes. When a troupe of dancers did their act in red costumes, complaints flooded in. On Baird's black and white TV, the dancers looked stark naked. Although it was a pioneering system, Baird's television eventually lost out to the much better one from Marconi EMI.

BEST SHOW IN TOWN?

Some top actors and performers didn't think the TV screen was the place to be seen in the 1930s. All pictures were black and white (in fact, they remained like this up until 1967).

Until September 1935, they were made up of only 30 lines so they were lousy in quality. By 1936, picture quality improved. Baird started making 240-line TV pictures and the company Marconi EMI started making pictures that had 405 lines. Even so, very few people actually saw any TV. By 1937, only 2000 TV sets had been sold and pictures were only broadcast to 56 kilometres away from the TV studio. Unlike today, if you were seen on TV you weren't automatically a household name. So it's no wonder the BBC had lots of problems getting top acts to appear on TV in the evenings. Many performers preferred to carry on with their usual 'live' shows in theatres and clubs.

NO WAY! I'M A TOP CLASS ACTOR!

BBC T.V.

SCRIPT

DRESS TO IMPRESS

Early presenters dressed just like the tiny, rich audience who could afford a TV set. The first TV sets were so expensive, they could only be enjoyed by the ultra-rich. Like most of their viewers, presenters dressed very smartly – in the evening they wore clothes that wouldn't look out of place at a formal dinner party. This genteel TV had a short life – TV broadcasts were stopped when war broke out in 1939. When TV came back after the war, it became something far less formal. Mind you, people on some programmes like the quiz show *What's my Line?*, carried on dressing up in smart, fancy clothes right up until the 1960s.

THE WRONG LINES

Did you know there's still a strict dress code on modern TV? These days, it's not the audience who won't like it if you turn up in the wrong clothes – but the camera crew. That's because certain patterns make a TV picture go haywire. A colour TV picture is broadcast by sending two pieces of information. One piece, called the 'chrominance', gives the colour of every part of the picture. The other piece, called the 'luminance', gives the brightness. If you wear clothes with loud, vertical stripes, these two signals get muddled when you move around. Your clothes will create a shimmering, rainbow effect that messes up the picture.

A BIGGER PICTURE

A bulging, see-through bowl was a good substitute for a big TV screen in the 1950s. The cost of a TV then was sky high – and most people couldn't afford anything with a large screen. Some manufacturers started selling see-through plastic bowls that you could put in front of a small screen to get a bigger picture.

Filled with a liquid called 'glycerine', they were often nicknamed 'goldfish bowls'. They made the picture bigger – but they also made it a little out of shape.

COLOUR TV

If you put a magnifying glass up to a modern TV screen, you'll see how it makes a colour picture. The TV picture is made up of thousands of tiny strips of separate colours: some green, some red and some blue. Our eyes blur these strips together to see a single, colour picture. Inside a colour TV there are three separate beams of electrons. Each one carries information about a different colour. Each strip on the screen can only be lit by one of these beams so only glows red, green or blue. Unless you are very close to the screen, your brain merges these dots together so you see a realistic, colour picture.

VIDEO RECORDERS

EARLY VIDEO

Video may look like a recent invention, but Baird had worked out how to record TV pictures as early as 1928. After a TV show is broadcast, it disappears forever, unless it is recorded. These days we usually record on video tape, but Baird was able to record his images on a gramophone record. Baird's system had so few lines (*see* **Line by line** *page 123*), it was fairly easy for him to record the pictures it made. His recordings never became popular – that's partly because they were so poor.

Researchers today have had to use really good computers to make the images he recorded look any good at all. Even with the help of a computer, they are not a patch on the quality of video today. Nevertheless, they do give us a vivid impression of the images Baird was creating in the early days of television.

TV DINNERS?

When you wanted to edit a videotape in 1955, you had to look under the microscope. Videotape recording was introduced in 1956 by the tape manufacturers Ampex. If you wanted to edit tape around this time, you had to paint it with a magnetic fluid. As the tape itself was covered in magnetic granules of rust, just like an audio tape (*see* **Not fade away** *page 56*), this fluid stuck to the tape in certain places only, showing the picture on the tape. This picture was so tiny, you could only see it under a microscope. This fiddly way of working with videos was called 'knife and fork' editing. Easy-to-use home video recorders didn't appear until 1972.

TAILORING THE TELLY

Imagine how handy it would be if all your favourite TV shows were on, only when you were in. Well, very soon, that could happen. It's already possible to buy a small box of tricks, called a 'set top box', that works a bit like a games console (*see* **Pong in the home** *page 109*). It lets you interact with your television. If you watch shows that have been made with a set top box in mind, you can press a few buttons to take part in quiz shows, find out more about tomorrow's TV and even look at the Internet (*see* **Home work** *page 77 and* **Web of war** *page 34*). Better still, you'll eventually be able to call up the programmes you missed and watch them when you're free. This service, called 'video on demand', could well spell the end of home video recorders.

SATELLITE BROADCASTING

OVER THEIR HEADS

Fortunately for science fiction fans, when a young engineer first suggested using satellites to send messages around the world, no one seemed remotely interested. That engineer was Arthur C. Clarke. In 1945, he wrote a short article for the magazine *Wireless World*, explaining how three satellites could bounce messages from any part of the world to another. After his ideas were completely ignored, he decided to try his hand at something new: writing science fiction books. Arthur C. Clarke went on to become one of the greatest writers of the century. Within twenty years of his article appearing, satellite communication had become the next big thing. In 1962, the satellite *Telstar* carried out some trial broadcasts of TV. By 1964, a satellite *Syncom III* was able to broadcast the Olympic Games from Tokyo, Japan, all the way to California, USA.

SILVER LINING

ECHO 1, the first communications satellite was nothing more than a big, silvery balloon. Launched by NASA in 1960, *ECHO 1* bounced radio waves from one part of the globe to another. NASA demonstrated *ECHO 1* by bouncing a recording of President Eisenhower's voice from California to New Jersey, USA. The quality of the received signal was so good, for a few seconds, that the engineers thought that they were listening to the recording before it had been transmitted.

ECHO 1 could only send one signal at a time, so its use was limited. However, it certainly helped to excite the general public about the coming of satellite communication. Many people fondly remember gazing at the great silvery balloon as it passed overhead, glistening at sunrise or sunset.

PAST COMES HOME TO ROOST

As the *ECHO 1* satellite was so crude, it unexpectedly led to an amazing discovery about the history of the universe. Scientists had to use very sensitive equipment to pick up the radio waves that bounced off the balloon. One day, while studying these signals, they noticed a steady, hissing signal that seemed to appear all the time, whether they used *ECHO 1* or not. After checking that the signal hadn't been caused by pigeons nesting in their receiver, two scientists, A.A. Penzias and R.W. Wilson, realised it was something altogether different. It was caused by the energy that was released during the Big Bang – the event that created the universe over fifteen billion years ago.

SATELLITE SPOTTING

If you look up to the sky on a clear night, you may be able to spot a satellite moving steadily overhead. The satellite seems to twinkle like a star as it reflects some of the Sun's rays back to Earth. These days, there are thousands of satellites littering Earth's orbit. We use them to carry TV, radio and mobile phone messages from one part of the world to another. Next time you watch a 'live' sports event, the images you see may well have travelled via satellite. Satellites are big business and rocket manufacturers often launch two or three satellites at a time. When the European Space Agency rocket *Ariane* exploded in 1996, millions of pounds worth of satellites were destroyed with it.

HISTORY LESSON

Hubble is a satellite that lets us look back in time. Launched on 24 April 1990, it carries a giant telescope that lets us see into the furthest reaches of the universe. As light takes over ten billion years to reach *Hubble* from such distant places, *Hubble* lets us see how the universe looked over ten billion years ago. After some initial teething problems (*see* **Fuzzy thinking** *page 108*), *Hubble* has given us glimpses of the births of stars and galaxies, vividly showing how the universe was probably formed.

MEDIA POWER

PRODUCT PLACEMENT

When a TV cook put whitebait in a recipe in 1951, shoppers stampeded to buy it and the price of the fish shot up overnight. This was one of the first times people had experienced the power of 'product placement'. TV advertising space is the most expensive around. As so many millions of people watch a top TV show, anything that appears on it, or on the adverts in the middle of it, gets far more coverage than it would on any billboard, magazine advertisement or supermarket shelf. What's more, if a favourite presenter says they like a product, viewers may be more tempted to buy it. It's no surprise then that TV programme makers have to be careful that they don't accidentally 'plug' a product on their show.

MEDIA REVOLUTION

These days when rebels want to overthrow the rulers of a country, their first stop is the television station. As television lets you communicate with millions, it's no wonder that it holds so much power. Lots of people find out what's going on in the world by watching the box. Whoever decides what gets shown on television can have a huge effect on what people know, think, see, buy – and even how they will vote. It's no wonder then that governments keep a close eye on what's shown on television – and who runs it.

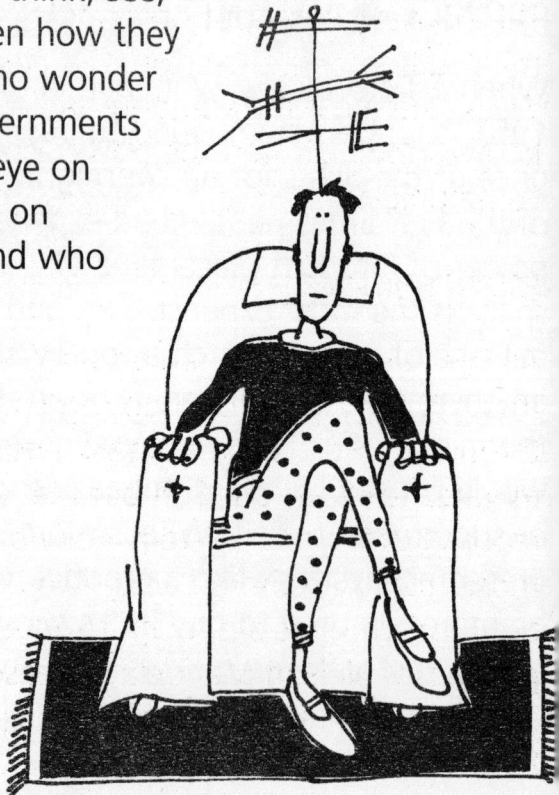

ALIEN ALERT

When a radio announcer interrupted some music to tell America that an army of aliens from Mars had landed, he caused widespread panic. His grave announcement, on 30 October 1938, was actually the beginning of a radio play – a gripping version of H.G. Well's science fiction masterpiece *War of the Worlds*. Unfortunately, many people who tuned in thought they were listening to a real broadcast. The US Navy were put on standby, taxis and train stations were overrun. Directed by Orson Wells, the most talked-about radio show ever had vividly illustrated the power of radio communication.

EARTH CALLING

All the television and radio ever broadcast through the airwaves is moving continually through space. TV signals take about eight minutes to reach our Sun but many years to reach another solar system. Early broadcasts, like those from Alexandra Palace, were very weak but modern ones are much stronger. Live pictures of Nelson Mandela's release from prison in 1990 will soon be reaching Sirius, a star over 83 billion kilometres away. Maybe an alien lifeform can tune into the incredibly tiny signals that are left after such a long journey. If so, they'll be able to watch and hear our old television and radio shows – and they'll certainly learn a lot about us.

Quiz

1 Centuries ago, British papers could only report
   a) royal stories
   b) serious stories
   c) foreign stories

2 As a young man, John Logie Baird tried to make a living selling
   a) footwarmers
   b) motorised roller-skates
   c) pet insurance

3 Shortly after Baird made his first TV picture he was
   a) evicted
   b) arrested
   c) knighted

4 When a troupe of dancers wore red on Baird's television, they seemed to be
   a) green
   b) floating
   c) naked

5 On modern TV, you should never wear
   a) a top hat
   b) a stripy shirt
   c) a personal stereo

6 By 1928, Baird had already found a way to
   a) record TV pictures
   b) operate a TV by remote control
   c) send Teletext messages

7 The first communications satellite was
   a) a high altitude aeroplane
   b) a spinning mirror
   c) a giant balloon

8 All the time, satellite receivers pick up a stray signal caused by
   a) the Big Bang
   b) dead pigeons
   c) other satellites

9 After a TV programme in 1951, people stampeded to buy
   a) a TV licence
   b) a fish
   c) a gas mask

10 In October 1938, there was widespread panic in America because people thought
   a) the president had been assassinated
   b) a volcano was about to erupt in New York
   c) the Martians had landed

Quiz Answers

CHAPTER 1 (PAGE 42)

1 - a,   2 - b,   3 - a,   4 - c,   5 - b,
6 - b,   7 - a,   8 - b,   9 - c,   10 - c

CHAPTER 2 (PAGE 62)

1 - b,   2 - a,   3 - a,   4 - b,   5 - a,
6 - b,   7 - a,   8 - a,   9 - b,   10 - c

CHAPTER 3 (PAGE 84)

1 - b,   2 - a,   3 - a, b and c (trick question)
4 - b,   5 - b,   6 - c,   7 - b,   8 - b,
9 - a,   10 - c

CHAPTER 4 (PAGE 113)

1 - b,   2 - a,   3 - c,   4 - a,   5 - a,
6 - c,   7 - b,   8 - a,   9 - a,   10 - c

CHAPTER 5 (PAGE 141)

1 - a,   2 - a,   3 - a,   4 - c,   5 - b,
6 - a,   7 - c,   8 - a,   9 - b,   10 - c

Index